YOUR CHOICE

A Personal Skills Course

MAKING DECISIONS
Shay McConnon and Margaret McConnon

Nelson

Thomas Nelson and Sons Ltd
Nelson House Mayfield Road
Walton-on-Thames Surrey
KT12 5PL UK

51 York Place
Edinburgh
EH1 3JD UK

Thomas Nelson (Hong Kong) Ltd
Toppan Building 10/F
22A Westlands Road
Quarry Bay Hong Kong

Thomas Nelson Australia
102 Dodds Street
South Melbourne
Vic 3205 Australia

Nelson Canada
1120 Birchmount Road
Scarborough Ontario
M1K 5G4 Canada

© Shay McConnon 1992

First Published by Thomas Nelson and Sons Ltd 1992

ISBN 0–17–420248–2
NPN 9 8 7 6 5 4 3 2

All rights reserved. No paragraph of this publication
may be reproduced, copied or transmitted save with
written permission or in accordance with the provisions
of the Copyright, Design and Patents Act 1988, or under
the terms of any licence permitting limited copying
issued by the Copyright Licensing Agency, 90 Tottenham
Court Road, London, W1P 9HE.

The photocopying of some pages is permitted. These pages
are marked thus Ⓟ. However, only reasonable quantities of
photocopies can be made and these should be for internal
school use only. Under no circumstances can large numbers
of copies be made either by schools or LEAs.

Any person who does any unauthorised act in relation to
this publication may be liable to criminal prosecution
and civil claims for damages.

Illustrated by Nick Oates, Nick Davies and Mike Akers

Printed in Great Britain by
Hobbs the Printers of Southampton

CONTENTS

Introduction		1
Profiling		3
Module Overview		6
1	Decisions	9
2	Which Way Is Best?	12
3	Making A Decision	14
4	Inform Yourself	20
5	What's Important To Me?	22
6	Solutions	26
7	Decide About Smoking	29
8	Decide About Alcohol	33
9	Decide About Drugs	37
10	Decide Your Career	41
11	Decide Your Subjects	43
12	Decide About...	45
13	How Have We Got On?	48

INTRODUCTION

Each day we make many decisions, some straightforward, even 'automatic', others difficult and requiring a lot of thought. Some are relatively unimportant; others can affect the rest of our lives.

This course teaches the skills for making satisfactory decisions. It is particularly relevant for young people who are experiencing greater freedom of choice and have (or will have) to make decisions about health, money, examinations, relationships, careers, politics, religion and other issues. It may also prevent teenagers from making decisions they will later regret: lung cancer can be the long-term consequence of a teenage decision to smoke.

Besides teaching the skills of decision making, the course provides opportunities for students to apply this decision-making process to real-life situations. Students are encouraged to take more control of their lives by taking responsibility for making considered and informed decisions.

Strategy 1

In the opening strategy students are helped to an awareness of the extent and range of decision making in their lives and also the importance of learning the skills for making effective decisions.

Strategies 2 - 3

Students evaluate different styles of decision making and identify those skills which are important for making an effective decision.

Strategies 4 - 6

The skills of gathering information, clarifying one's values and generating alternative solutions are examined in detail as essential steps in the decision-making process.

Strategies 7 - 9

Students now use the skills of decision making to make an informed and considered decision about smoking, alcohol and illicit drugs.

Strategies 10 - 11

Students use the decision-making strategy to help them to clarify a choice of career and subject options.

Strategies 12 - 13

Students make decisions to help them achieve greater personal effectiveness. Finally there is an evaluation of the students' response to this course on decisions.

Most of the strategies involve group work. The group can be the teacher's most effective resource in helping students to become aware of their ability to make effective decisions. The group also provides opportunities to experiment with new behaviours and receive feedback on them. Such work, however, requires sensitive handling by the teacher, who needs to create a positive, non-critical atmosphere in which individuals feel valued and listened to.

The time suggested for each strategy is an approximate guideline. The ability and maturity of the students will determine how long each strategy takes. Each strategy is divided into several phases which provide a natural break for limited time sessions. Most strategies include ideas for variations on the main procedure or a development of the exercise. Although the exercises are suitable across a wide age range, the teacher might wish to modify the content to make them more relevant to a specific group.

PROFILING

Recent initiatives in education encourage a move towards profiling, continuous assessment and reviewing. Assessment is to be seen as an integral part of all learning experiences. The student is at the centre of this process and its success requires that students understand the assessment process. Giving students a copy of their profile statements at the beginning of the course allows them to become aware of the assessment objectives. By explaining these objectives and the assessment procedure, students will know what to assess themselves on and how.

The review is a key element in effective profiling. Ideally this should take place at regular intervals during the course, rather than leaving the review to the end.

The completed worksheets could be used to form part of the student's formative profile and provide useful moments for reviewing with the student.

The teacher may wish to involve parents in this process and design the profile to allow them to make written comments.

The teacher could also design a scheme which asks students to assess themselves at the end of each session, e.g.

	Sessions							
	1	2	3	4	5	6	7	8
I work without supervision	8	6	9					
I work to the best of my ability	7	5						
I am keen to learn	7	7						

Students score themselves out of ten for each of these skill areas. Over a period of time, students will get a picture of themselves and be able to note areas of success along with skills needing attention. This can be reviewed with the teacher.

However the profile is designed or executed, students hopefully will feel that their formative profiles are a tool they can use to become more aware of self, to monitor progress and decide on new starting points.

The profile statement which follows is in two parts. (A) is an assessment sheet for skills taught during the course. (B) is an assessment sheet for students' attitudes and their ability to co-operate with each other. Each sheet allows both teacher and student to make independent comments on progress. These can be used as a basis for a review resulting in a joint comment.

PROFILE STATEMENT (A): DECISIONS

Name _____

Date _____

		COMMENTS
1	I am aware of decision-making styles (both helpful and unhelpful).	
2	I know what skills are important in making a satisfactory decision.	
3	I can use these decision-making skills:	
	- I can assess what I need to know and then get this information.	
	- I have a clear idea of my values (what is important to me).	
	- I can think of different solutions and weigh up their advantages and disadvantages.	
4	I can use this strategy to make informed and considered decisions:	
	- About smoking.	
	- About alcohol.	
	- About illicit drugs.	
	- About my career and future.	
	- About my choice of subjects.	

STUDENT

Report on the progress you have made:

TEACHER

Report on this student's progress:

JOINT COMMENTS

After discussion, we have agreed that progress has been made in:

But attention needs to be paid to:

The following action has been agreed on:

Signed _____ TEACHER

Signed _____ STUDENT

℗ © Shay McConnon 1992

PROFILE STATEMENT (B) : DECISIONS

Name _____ Date _____

ATTITUDE AND WORKING WITH OTHERS

> Indicate your attitude by marking the continuum line with an X.
> The teacher will score your attitude on this line with an O.

	ALWAYS	SOMETIMES	NEVER
I work without supervision.			
I work to the best of my ability.			
I am keen to learn.			
I organise myself.			
I make good use of the time available.			
I co-operate with other students.			
I try to involve the quieter members.			
I make suggestions and offer ideas.			
I listen attentively to others.			
I help the group make decisions.			
I talk with confidence in the group.			
I try to understand other students' points of view.			

What I do well is:

What I could do better is:

℗ © Shay McConnon 1992

MODULE OVERVIEW

CHAPTER	DESCRIPTION	TYPE OF ACTIVITY	TIME	SIZE OF GROUP	WORK-SHEETS	ADDITIONAL MATERIALS	WORK EXTENSION
1 Decisions	Students are helped to an awareness of the extent and range of decision making in their lives.	brainstorming	30	4 - 6, pairs	1	paper and markers	✓
2 Which Way Is Best?	Students identify and evaluate different styles of decision making.	rank-ordering	30	3 - 4	1	–	✓
3 Making A Decision	The skills for making effective decisions are identified.	skill identification	30 - 40	3 - 4	4	–	✓
4 Inform Yourself	Students examine the importance of gathering information and then analysing it critically.	information seeking	30	3 - 4	1	–	✓
5 What's Important To Me?	The link between personal values and decision making is established and students are given the opportunity to identify their values.	value clarification	30 - 40	pairs	2	–	✓
6 Solutions	Students consider the skills of identifying alternatives and then weighing up their advantages and disadvantages.	brainstorming	30	5 - 6	1	paper and markers	✓
7 Decide About Smoking	Students use the decision-making strategy to make an informed and considered decision about tobacco.	decision making	40 - 50	5 - 6, 2 - 6	2	paper and markers	✓

MODULE OVERVIEW

CHAPTER	DESCRIPTION	TYPE OF ACTIVITY	TIME	SIZE OF GROUP	WORK-SHEETS	ADDITIONAL MATERIALS	WORK-EXTENSION
8 Decide About Alcohol	Using the skills of decision making, students make a personal decision about where they stand on the issue of alcohol.	decision making	40 - 50	5 - 6, 2 - 6	2	paper and markers	✓
9 Decide About Drugs	Students make an informed and considered decision about illicit drugs.	decision making	40 - 50	5 - 6, 2 - 6	2	paper and markers	✓
10 Decide Your Career	Students apply the skills of decision making to help them decide on a career.	decision making	30 - 40	5 - 6, 3 - 4	1	paper and markers	✓
11 Decide Your Subjects	Students use the skills of decision making to make an informed and considered decision about subject options.	decision making	30 - 40	5 - 6	1	paper and markers	✓
12 Decide About...	Students use the decision-making strategy to help them achieve greater personal effectiveness.	decision making	30 - 40	3 - 4	2	–	✓
13 How Have We Got On?	An assessment of the student's response to this course.	evaluation	30 - 40	varies	1	–	✓

1 DECISIONS

Aim: To help students become aware of the extent and range of decision making in their lives.

Procedure:

• Phase I
- Form groups of 4 - 6 and give each a large sheet of paper and a marker.
- Each group decides on a spokesperson and a secretary.
- Students brainstorm on 'decisions made since getting up this morning'.
- The secretary lists these on the sheet of paper.
- Allow approximately five minutes for this.
- Each group goes through its list, putting a tick beside those decisions which were made automatically (i.e. requiring little or no thought) and a cross beside those decisions which people found more difficult to make (i.e. those which required more thought and investigation).
- Convene the class and ask each spokesperson to report back on three decisions which were automatically made and three decisions which required some thought.
- Discuss:
  – Were people surprised by the number of decisions they had made already today?
  – Which decisions were difficult to make?
  – Why were these decisions difficult?
  – Has anyone made decisions they have regretted? Examples?
  – How important is it to learn an effective way of making decisions? (The teacher could use this moment to give an outline of the course on decision making and its relevance to the pupils' lives.)

• Phase II
- Give each student the worksheet **DECISIONS**.
- This may be completed individually or with a partner of the student's choosing.
- Students then share their completed worksheet with a partner they have not worked with.
- Invite students to report on the important decisions they have to make in the near future.
- List these on the blackboard or flipchart.
- Discuss:
  – During which period in our lives do we probably have most choice and hence the opportunity to make many decisions?
  – During which period of our lives do we probably have least choice and hence the opportunity to make few decisions?

Group Size: 4 - 6, pairs

Time: 30 minutes

Materials: Each student requires:
- the worksheet **DECISIONS**

Each group requires:
- a large sheet of paper and a marker

  – How do you rate the present period in your lives? How much opportunity do you have for making decisions?
  – What decisions do young people have to make which might affect the rest of their lives (e.g. smoking)?
  – Do boys make decisions more easily than girls?
  – Are people instinctively good decision makers or is it a skill that can be learned?

Extensions:

1. Students analyse the number of decisions they have to make in a given situation, e.g. MY JOURNEY TO SCHOOL or A MATHS LESSON.
2. Phase I can be varied by asking students to categorise their list of decisions into important and unimportant decisions.
3. Ask for a volunteer to talk to the class about a major decision he has to make and explain why and how he is hoping to go about making that decision.
4. Students list five decisions typical for a 10 year old, a 15 year old, a 20 year old, and a 40 year old and finally for a 60 year old.
5. Explore the idea of influences (peer pressure, advertisements, etc.) in making decisions. Students could list the influences that are particularly relevant to young people and their decision making.

Notes:

Decision making is part of life. Some decisions are 'automatic' and uncomplicated (tying my shoelace); others are difficult and require some thought (what job shall I try for when I leave school). Some decisions are unimportant (to have chips or mash with my lunch) others affect the rest of our lives (to smoke or remain a non-smoker).

This opening strategy encourages students to become aware of the time they spend in decision making whether they are conscious of having to make all the decisions or not. It also allows students to differentiate between decisions which are 'automatic' and those requiring thought and investigation.

The brainstorm (Phase I) will work best if all the ideas offered are written down without any criticism or evaluative comments.

The 'important decision I will have to make in the near future' which students have written on their worksheets could be printed in bold letters on strips of coloured paper or card and displayed on the classroom walls for the duration of the course. These can be used during the course when examples of decision making are required for the identification and practice of decision-making skills.

DECISIONS

Name _____ Date _____

List ten decisions you make in a typical day.

What clothes shall I wear?

What present shall I get for Mum's birthday?

1. _____
2. _____
3. _____
4. _____
5. _____
6. _____
7. _____
8. _____
9. _____
10. _____

Shall I watch TV or do homework?

Shall I smoke?

Shall I return home at the agreed time?

What shall I eat for lunch?

Shall I lie in?

How shall I spend my pocket money?

Note the two most important decisions:

1. _____
2. _____

Note the two most difficult decisions:

1. _____
2. _____

I find it difficult to make decisions. ⊢——┴——┴——┴——⊣ I find it easy to make decisions.

I have a lot of choice/ control in my life. ⊢——┴——┴——┴——⊣ I have little choice/ control in my life.

Three important decisions I will have to make in the near future are:

1. _____
2. _____
3. _____

© Shay McConnon 1992

2 WHICH WAY IS BEST?

Aim: To help students become aware of different styles of decision making and to evaluate these.

Procedure:

- **Phase I**
  - Give each student the worksheet **WHICH WAY IS BEST?**
  - Read through the task in Section A and allow time for students to complete this without reference to others.
  - Convene the class and discuss:
    - Who was able to make their decision quickly?
    - Did many change their minds?
    - Was everyone satisfied with the way they made their decisions? Why? Why not?
    - How did people go about making their decisions?
    - What would have helped you make a satisfactory decision about a personal stereo?

- **Phase II**
  - Students are asked to think about how they usually make decisions and then complete Section B of the worksheet by circling those comments on the sheet which apply to them.
  - In groups of 3 - 4, students take it in turns to talk about their style of decision making.

- **Phase III**
  - Each student now completes Section C of the worksheet by putting the list of decision-making styles in rank order - the most effective form of decision making scores 1.
  - In their groups of 3 - 4, students are to agree on the two most satisfactory ways for making decisions.
  - Convene the class and invite each group to report back on what they considered the two most satisfactory ways for making decisions.
  - Discuss:
    - What are generally considered satisfactory ways for making decisions?
    - What are generally considered unsatisfactory ways for making decisions?
    - Is there one best way, or should different styles be used to suit different situations? Examples?
    - What do we mean by a 'bad' decision?
    - What do we mean by a 'good' decision?
    - What are the common mistakes in making decisions?

Group Size: 3 - 4

Time: 30 minutes

Materials: Each student requires:
- the worksheet **WHICH WAY IS BEST?**

Notes:

Having established that decision making plays a major part in our lives, the course now progresses to an examination of how we actually make decisions.

The session opens with a decision-making task. Students are asked to reflect on this and other decision-making experiences and identify their own style of decision making. Several such styles are evaluated and conclusions drawn about their suitability.

The task in Phase I lacks the necessary information for students to reach a satisfactory decision (though some students may know a lot about personal stereos - prices, specifications, features, etc.). The intention is not that students necessarily make an informed decision but that they become aware of how they approach decision making. This will lay the foundations for future sessions when the skills for making effective decisions will be identified and practised.

Extensions:

1. Conclude Phase III by asking students in their small groups to agree to the two least satisfactory ways for making decisions.
2. Students write the names of three people who influence them and the decisions they make. They then list the type of situations in which they might turn to these people for help and the reasons why these people might influence them.
3. Invite students to explore the effect of advertising on decision making... TV adverts, teenage magazines, and so on. Why are the images so glamorous? Do adverts give a balanced picture? Can they be misleading?

WHICH WAY IS BEST?

Name _____ Date _____

SECTION A

You are the only person in your group of friends who does not own a personal stereo. You win £100 in a raffle and at last you have the money for your own personal stereo. Decide on a model, the features you require, the colour you like and the money you are prepared to spend.

MODEL _____

COLOUR _____

COST _____

FEATURES _____

SECTION B

Circle the comments which apply to your style of decision making.

I weigh up all the pros and cons.

I ask other people their opinion.

I can never make up my mind.

I go along with what everyone else thinks.

I just panic.

I do nothing and hope someone else will make the decision for me.

I get confused and cannot think straight.

I make a decision just to please others.

I keep putting it off.

I worry about what other people will think about my decision.

I do whatever my parents advise.

I think it through.

I toss a coin.

I trust my instincts.

It doesn't matter what I think or decide.

I gather as much information as possible before making a decision.

I just know what is best.

SECTION C

Rank-order this list of decision-making styles. The most satisfactory way scores a one.

	Toss a coin and decide.
	Go along with what others decide.
	Do nothing but wait and see what happens.
	Make a decision to please others.
	No need to think; just do what feels right.
	Think everything through before making a decision.
	Do the first thing that comes into your head.

© Shay McConnon 1992

MAKING A DECISION

Aim: To help students to identify the skills required for making satisfactory decisions.

Procedure:
• Phase I
- Form groups of 3 - 4.
- Give each group a set of **MAKING A DECISION CARDS** and explain the task:
  – Each group is to select and arrange in order, those cards which are important to making a 'good' decision. The set contains cards which are not relevant to making a decision.
  – The bogus cards are those on the right-hand side of the sheet. The cards on the left-hand side are set out in the correct order (top to bottom) for making a 'good' decision.
- When the task has been completed, invite groups to report back their conclusions.
- Write on the blackboard or flipchart the steps to effective decision making and comment on these (see Notes).

• Phase II
- Give each student a copy of **THE "WHAT" REPORT**.
- Explain that this sheet should help students to make a more informed decision about a personal stereo (continuing the task set in the previous exercise).
- Give each student a copy of **MAKING A DECISION ABOUT A PERSONAL STEREO** and explain how it is to be completed.
  – To INFORM YOURSELF you can read **THE "WHAT" REPORT**, and talk to friends who own a personal stereo.
  – The section BE CLEAR ABOUT WHAT IS IMPORTANT TO YOU asks students to decide between sound quality, radio reception, price and other features of the stereos available.
- Students now complete this sheet using the information in **THE "WHAT" REPORT**.
- In their groups of 3 - 4, students take it in turns to share their completed worksheets. Convene the class and discuss:
  – Was it easier to make a satisfactory decision (than in the previous exercise)?
  – Why was this?
  – Did people feel that the steps outlined on the sheet helped them to make a more satisfactory decision?

Group Size: 3 - 4

Time: 30 - 40 minutes

Materials: Each student requires:
- the worksheets **THE "WHAT" REPORT** and **MAKING A DECISION ABOUT A PERSONAL STEREO**

Each group requires:
- a set of **MAKING A DECISION CARDS**

– Which parts of the process were easy/difficult to apply?
– Did people still find it difficult to make a final choice? Why was this?
– What are the important elements in making a satisfactory decision?

Extensions:
1. In pairs, students identify a decision they have to make which is causing some concern. Students take it in turns to help each other to use the decision-making process to make the best possible decision. Students may use the **MAKING A DECISION** sheet.
2. Extend the decision-making process outlined to include a review of the decision itself, i.e. having made the decision, act on it and then check to see if it worked. If not, what new solution could be tried?
3. Give a weighting (0-10) to each of the advantages and disadvantages listed in Step Five of the **MAKING A DECISION** sheet. Total the points for each to give an impression of which outweighs the other.

Notes:

Having explored the different ways people make decisions, the course progresses to an analysis of the skills (steps) involved in making an effective decision.

Students are given the opportunity to reflect on a decision-making process, become aware of the skills involved, order these and finally apply these skills to a situation which requires a decision to be made.

For the purposes of this course, a six step decision-making process is described. The intention has been to keep this process simple and workable.

Step 1 is to describe the situation, i.e. recognise what decision has to be made. (e.g. Which personal stereo do I want to buy?)

Step 2 is to gather information: find out the facts, check with other people, ask opinions, read reports, and so on. The more information we have the easier it will probably be to make a 'good' decision)e.g. I read **THE "WHAT" REPORT** and check out with my friends who own personal stereos.)

Step 3 is to be clear about what is important to me. A satisfactory decision will reflect my values and goals. This step helps the student clarify his values in so far as they are relevant to this decision. (e.g. Sound quality is important to me and I want to use my stereo when I go jogging.)

It now becomes easier to consider solutions which is **Step 4**. (e.g. Susi and Toshi are the only two models which incorporate good sound quality and are suitable for jogging.)

Step 5 is to think about the advantages and disadvantages of each solution and consider the consequences. This is an important step and help can be sought from others in looking at alternatives. (Toshi is more expensive than Susi but it comes with in-ear headphones. Susi is bigger and heavier but has auto-reverse.)

Step 6 is to make the decision based on your research and personal reflection (e.g. 'I shall buy the Toshi model.')

There are two worksheets called **MAKING A DECISION**. One has clues which are relevant to making a decision about a personal stereo and is to be used in this exercise. The other has no clues and can be used as a guide for students in their decision making about other issues.

MAKING A DECISION

THE 'WHAT' REPORT

PERSONAL STEREO 'SPECIALS'

Type	Target price	Accessories supplied	Weight	Size	Features	Ease of use	Sound quality	Radio reception	Running cost	Jogging
	£									
WAWI (S-T1)	80	YZ	II	II	AB	★	★	✦	£	✧
SONA (CP-5)	60	XY	III	III	BC	★	⊛	★	£	✦
TOSHI (RX-A5)	85	VXYZ	I	I	BD	⊛	✦	✦	££	✦
REAL (F-107)	70	XY	II	II	BC	⊛	✦	✦	£	★
SULAR (KT-41)	70	WXY	III	III	ABC	⊛	✦	★	££	☆
SUSANI (FX-51)	60	YZ	III	II	AB	★	✦	✦	£	★
HIBA (SC-43)	100	VWXY	II	I	ABCD	⊛	⊛	★	££	✦
SUSI (HS-8)	80	VXY	III	III	AB	★	✦	★	£	✦
NUSSI (R2-5)	70	WXY	II	II	BC	✦	☆	✦	£	★
SONIC (TK-101)	50	WY	II	II	BC	✦	✧	✦	£	★

TABLE GUIDE

Ease of use:
Tests included how easy it was to change a cassette or batteries and to use the radio features.

Sound quality:
Tests were carried out with a variety of audio tapes and the ratings take account of motor noise and base/treble reproduction.

Radio reception:
The ratings are based on laboratory tests and reception trials for VHF wavelengths.

Running costs:
The ratings are based on the amount of electric current used during tape play, using two LR6 SUPERPOWER batteries.

Jogging:
Tests showed that the sound quality suffered with the jolting caused by jogging. Some sets were lighter, easier to carry and more suitable for jogging.

WARNING

It's dangerous to cycle or cross the road if your personal stereo means you can't hear traffic noise or other warnings.
Listening at high volume levels - especially for long periods - can permanently damage your hearing.

KEY TO RATINGS   ✦ ✧ ★ ☆ ⊛

← best   worst →

Features:
A = auto-reverse (switches to other side at end of cassette)
B = independent volume adjustment of left and right earpieces
C = connection for playback through other audio equipment
D = 4-band graphic equalizer

Accessories supplied:
V = belt clip
W = wrist-strap
X = case
Y = on-ear headphones
Z = in-ear headphones

Key to weight (with batteries):
I = less than 250g
II = 250 to 350g
III = 350 to 400g

Key to size:
I = 11 x 8 x 3cm
II = 12 x 8 x 3•5cm
III = 14 x 9 x 3•5cm

Key to running cost:
£ = 3 to 5p an hour
££ = 10 to 12p an hour

Shay McConnon 1992

MAKING A DECISION - CARDS

State the decision to be made.	**Explain your thinking.**
Inform yourself.	**Get permission.**
Be clear about what is important to you.	**Consider the risks.**
List solutions.	**Make a back-up plan.**
Think about advantages/ disadvantages.	**Check that time is available.**
Make a decision.	

© Shay McConnon 1992

MAKING A DECISION ABOUT A PERSONAL STEREO

Name _____ Date _____

1 What is the decision to be made?
_____

2 Inform yourself (read reports, talk to friends, etc.)
_____
_____
_____

3 Be clear about what is important to you (sound quality, radio reception, price, accessories, etc.)
_____
_____
_____

4 List solutions (i.e. the three models which are most suitable)

a _____

b _____

c _____

5 Think about advantages and disadvantages of each model.

SOLUTIONS	ADVANTAGES	DISADVANTAGES
A		
B		
C		

6 MAKE A DECISION

My decision is: _____

MAKING A DECISION

MAKING A DECISION

Name _____ Date _____

1 What is the decision to be made?
_____
_____

2 Inform yourself.
_____
_____
_____
_____

3 Be clear about what is important to you.
_____
_____
_____
_____

4 List solutions

a _____

b _____

c _____

5 Think about advantages/disadvantages/outcomes.

	SOLUTIONS	ADVANTAGES	DISADVANTAGES	LIKELY OUTCOMES
A				
B				
C				

6 MAKE A DECISION

My decision is: _____

© Shay McConnon 1992

4 INFORM YOURSELF!

Aim: To help students become aware of the importance of information to making satisfactory decisions.

Procedure:

• Phase I
- Recap on the steps to making a decision and in particular on the importance of informing oneself.
- Give each student the worksheet **INFORM YOURSELF!**
- Students ask themselves whether they would require a lot, some or little information before they could make a satisfactory decision about the situations listed and then tick the relevant box.
- Students form groups of 3 - 4 and share answers.
- If there is disagreement, students should justify their choice.
- Convene the class and discuss:
  - Did people find this task easy or difficult?
  - Was there much agreement in the answers?
  - Is this to be expected?
  - Why?

• Phase II
- Students now complete the next section of the worksheet, i.e. for each of the situations listed they decide what information will be required before making a satisfactory decision and how this information can be obtained.
- Students may work individually or in self-selecting groups.
- Finally, students identify a decision they have to make and how the necessary information can be obtained, and record this on the worksheet.
- Students share their worksheets in groups of 3 - 4.
- Convene the class and discuss:
  - What part does information play in making decisions?
  - What type of decisions require a lot of information?
  - Is it possible to have too much information (i.e. can too much data lead to confusion)? Examples?
  - Would anyone like to tell the class of a poor decision they made because they did not inform themselves?

Extensions:
1. Ask students to brainstorm decisions that young people have to make. These should be 'sorted' into decisions that require a lot of information, some and little.

Group Size: 3 - 4
Time: 30 minutes
Materials: Each student requires:
- the worksheet **INFORM YOURSELF!**

Notes:
The course now examines the various steps to effective decision making that have been identified in the previous session. This strategy focuses on the importance of information to making a satisfactory decision.

Our decision making will be limited if we do not take the trouble to collect information and examine it critically. Without this preparation decisions may be regretted. Not all decisions require in-depth information and, indeed, data overload can lead to confusion rather than clarity.

This session begins with students differentiating between decisions which require a lot of information and those which require little information, proceeds to look at the sources of information for decision-making and finally invites students to apply this process of information gathering to decisions they are to make.

The teacher may wish to give additional examples of information gathering to the one outlined on the sheet **INFORM YOURSELF!**

2. In small groups, students take it in turns to give examples from their own lives of poor decisions made because of a lack of information.

INFORM YOURSELF!

Name _____
Date _____

Ask yourself whether you would require a lot, some, or little information before you could make a satisfactory decision about each of the situations listed. Then tick the relevant box.

	A LOT	SOME	LITTLE
To smoke or not			
What to wear			
Which video to hire			
How to spend my money			
To become a vegetarian			
Which personal stereo to buy			
The job I would like			

	A LOT	SOME	LITTLE
What to eat for breakfast			
The type of person I would like to marry			
To open a savings account			
To take illicit drugs			
To leave or stay on at school			
Which holiday to go on			
Which TV channel to watch			

Information helps us to make 'good' decisions. Fill in the boxes for the following situations. The first is completed as an example for you.

Situation	What information do I require? (questions to be asked)	How can I get this information? (how can these questions be answered?)
Someone offers to sell me a radio cassette for £30. It is only a month old and cost £90 new.	1 Does it work? 2 Why is it so cheap? 3 Is it a good brand name? 4 Can this person be trusted?	1 Test the radio cassette by playing it. 2 Ask the person. 3 Check in the shops and magazines. 4 Ask your friends or people who know him.
A birthday present for Mum	1 _____ 2 _____ 3 _____	1 _____ 2 _____ 3 _____
The job I want when I leave school	1 _____ 2 _____ 3 _____	1 _____ 2 _____ 3 _____

Complete the section below for a decision you have to make.

A decision I have to make: _____	1 _____ 2 _____ 3 _____	1 _____ 2 _____ 3 _____

© Shay McConnon 1992

5 WHAT'S IMPORTANT TO ME?

Aim: To help students become aware of the importance of personal values to decision making.

Procedure:

• Phase I
- Explain to the class that you are going to ask them to make some decisions and then reflect on these to see what they have learned about themselves and their values. Would you rather have:
  - A sense of humour?
  - Good looks?
  - An IQ of 140?

  You can only choose one.
- Hands up:
  - Those who would rather have a sense of humour.
  - Those who would choose good looks.
  - Finally those who would choose an IQ of 140.
- Repeat with the following choice between:
  - Being the prime minister/a pop star/representing your country in the Olympic games.
  - Having £10,000/lots of friends/an adventure trip around the world.
- Briefly discuss:
  - What have we learnt about ourselves in making these decisions?
  - What do decisions tell us about the person making that decision?
  - Our decisions reflect our values (i.e. what is important to us). Do you agree or disagree?

• Phase II
- Give each student a copy of **WHAT'S IMPORTANT TO ME? (1)**.
- Explain the task and how the worksheet is to be completed.
- When the students have filled in the worksheets, form pairs for the students to take it in turns to share their answers.
- Briefly discuss:
  - Are we more likely to make satisfactory decisions if we are aware of our values? Why? Examples?
  - How do we become more aware of our values?

• Phase III
- Give each student a copy of **WHAT'S IMPORTANT TO ME? (2)**.
- Comment on the various sections and how they are to be completed.

Group Size: pairs

Time: 30 - 40 minutes

Materials: Each student requires:
- the worksheets **WHAT'S IMPORTANT TO ME 1** and **2**

- After students have completed the worksheets, they form pairs and exchange sheets.
- Each student studies his partner's sheet and writes a paragraph on VALUES WHICH APPEAR IMPORTANT TO...
- Allow time for students to complete this.
- Students now take it in turns to share their conclusions with their partners.
- Convene the class and discuss:
  - Why is it important for you to be aware of your values?
  - How does this clarity help decision making?

Extensions:

1. During Phase III, invite students not only to identify their partner's values (from studying her/his completed worksheet) but also to list some decisions she or he might make based on these values.
2. Reflecting on their completed worksheet **WHAT'S IMPORTANT TO ME? (2)**, students select a personal value of particular importance to them and trace the impact this value has on their lives - why it is important, how they came to value it, the ways it shows in their lives, and so on.
3. THE VALUE AUCTION or THE LIFE GAME from the *Your Choice* unit on *Self Awareness* can be used to heighten students' awareness of their value system.
4. Students list 10 decisions they have made in the past month and identify the values reflected in these decisions.

Notes:

Without a clear sense of what is important to me it will be difficult for me to make satisfactory decisions. The chances of making a 'sound' decision increases if I am clear about my values. The dilemma of whether to visit my Nan or go with my friends to the disco will be helped by being clear about which is more important to me: my Nan's feelings, a fun evening, loyalty to my friends, etc.

The strategy opens by exploring the link between decisions and values - how decisions reflect the values we hold. Students are given an opportunity to become aware of their personal values in Phase III and this should help them with their decision making.

Students may struggle in completing the worksheet **WHAT'S IMPORTANT TO ME? (2)** and may benefit from the teacher giving an example of a completed sheet. The teacher may wish to treat this as a private exercise (perhaps as homework) rather than ask students to share what could be considered personal and private.

WHAT'S IMPORTANT TO ME? (1)

Name _____ Date _____

A person who decides to be a non-smoker values:
_____

The teenager who returns home at the agreed time values:
_____

A person who spends lots of money on fashion clothes values:
_____

A person who values his health might decide to:
_____

A person who values friendship might decide to:
_____

A person who values power might decide to:
_____

You have just discovered that your classmate Tom has been stealing from Woolworths. What would you do?

- tell Tom he is an idiot
- keep quiet
- try to help him
- tell Tom's parents
- help him to steal next time
- go to the police

What is your decision?
_____
_____

What values does this reflect?
_____
_____

On the way home from school, your two best friends invite you to go to the disco. You agree. Only when you get home do you remember you had already promised to visit your Nan that evening. Your Nan lives on her own.

What is your decision?
_____
_____

What values does this reflect?
_____
_____

© Shay McConnon 1992

WHAT'S IMPORTANT TO ME? (2)

Name _____ Date _____

You have been invited to take part in a space mission. You are allowed one suitcase for personal possessions (food and survival items are provided). What do you take?

1 _____
2 _____
3 _____
4 _____
5 _____
6 _____

People I admire a lot are:
(these may be living or dead, famous or unknown)

Name	Reasons I admire this person
1 _____	_____
2 _____	_____
3 _____	_____

If I discovered I had only another month to live, these things would be important for me to do.

_____
_____
_____
_____
_____

Complete these sentences

I am happy when _____

I am proud that I _____

I am sad when _____

© Shay McConnon 1992

6 SOLUTIONS

Aim: To introduce students to the decision-making skills of generating different solutions and then evaluating these.

Procedure:

• Phase I
- Explain that one of the key skills in making sound decisions is the ability to generate alternative solutions to the problem and then consider the advantages/disadvantages of each.
- Form groups of 5 - 6 and decide on a spokesperson and secretary.
- Give each group a large sheet of paper and a marker.
- Each group is to list as many uses as they can think of for a packet of playing cards.
- The group with the longest list is the winner.
- Allow three minutes for this.
- Convene the class and ask each group to report back.
- Invite the winning group to suggest reasons why they had the longest list.
- Discuss with the class:
  - How can solutions/alternatives be generated?
  - What happens if someone is critical or dismissive of other people's ideas?
  - Should 'crazy' or far-out ideas be considered?
  - Is it important that everyone contributes?

• Phase II
- Give each group the worksheet **TONY'S PROBLEM** and a large sheet of paper.
- Read aloud Tony's problem and ask each group to use the skills of brainstorming identified in Phase I to generate ideas on how Tony could solve his problem.
- After approximately five minutes, each group selects the three best ways for solving Tony's problem and the secretary lists these on the worksheet.
- Taking each solution in turn, groups identify the advantages, disadvantages and likely outcomes and score the chances of success out of ten.
- These are written on the worksheet.
- Each group takes it in turns to report back and students should be prepared to answer questions asked by the class.
- Convene the class and discuss:
  - Is brainstorming for solutions a good idea?
  - How can you select the solution which would be best?
  - How can looking at the advantages/ disadvantages/consequences help?
  - Would it be helpful for us to use this approach when making a difficult decision?

Group Size: 5 - 6

Time: 30 minutes

Materials: Each group requires:
- a large sheet of paper and a marker
- the worksheet **TONY'S PROBLEM**

- Repeat the above procedure with the following situation.

> You are having a great time at the disco and must leave to be home at the time you agreed with your parents. Your friends encourage you to stay. What is your decision?

Extensions:

1. Students apply this process to a decision they have to make. This can be done in small self-selecting groups with students helping each other.
2. The teacher may wish to extend Phase II by providing students with further examples of decisions to be made. Here are some situations which can be used:
   a) Sheila is teased because she has just started to wear glasses.
   b) Some boys are making fun of John who is timid and shy.
   c) Paul is teased because he is too fat and not able to run fast enough at football.
   d) Jane has not many friends and complains of being bored and having nothing to do.

Notes:

People who are skilled in decision making consider consequences and risks before reaching a conclusion. They inform themselves about alternatives and identify advantages and disadvantages of each. In this way risk is minimised and the likelihood of desirable outcomes increased.

Phase I introduces students to the idea of brainstorming. Although students may have already used this technique in other strategies, it is important that they identify what constitutes a successful brainstorm.

Brainstorming is a way of listing as many solutions as possible in a short period of time. All the ideas offered (even the far-out ones) should be accepted and written down. No criticism or evaluative comments should be made. The emphasis is to be on quantity not quality.

Phase II allows students to practise brainstorming solutions for specific problems and then evaluate these solutions. This is one of the key skills in making satisfactory decisions.

TONY'S PROBLEM

Tony is unhappy. He doesn't get as much pocket money as his friends and when his money runs out he makes excuses not to go with them. He doesn't want to 'scrounge' but would like to spend more time with his mates. What can he do?

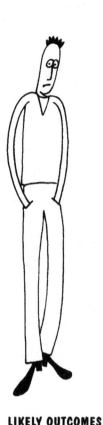

	SOLUTIONS	ADVANTAGES	DISADVANTAGES	LIKELY OUTCOMES
a)				
b)				
c)				

© Shay McConnon 1992

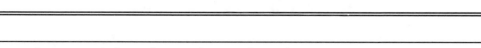

DECIDE ABOUT SMOKING

Aim: To help students make an informed and considered decision about smoking, using the decision-making strategy from this course.

Procedure:

• Phase I
- Form groups of 5 - 6 and decide on a spokesperson and secretary.
- Give each group a large sheet of paper and a marker.
- Students are to brainstorm the reasons why people choose to smoke, i.e. what is important to them in deciding to smoke.
- When this has been done, invite each group to report back and make a list of these responses on the blackboard or flipchart.
- Repeat this procedure, brainstorming the reasons why people choose not to smoke, i.e. what is important to them in deciding not to smoke.

• Phase II
- Form six groups (each group to consist of 2 - 6 students).
- Each group decides on a spokesperson and secretary.
- Give each group the worksheet **FACTS ABOUT SMOKING** and explain that they may use this to complete the next task.
- Give each group a large sheet of paper and a marker.
- Groups 1 and 2 will consider the choice NOT TO SMOKE and the secretary writes this at the top of the sheet.
- Groups 3 and 4 will consider TO SMOKE A LITTLE (restrict myself) and write this at the top of the sheet.
- Groups 5 and 6 will consider TO SMOKE A LOT (no limits) and write this at the top of the sheet.
- Groups 1, 3 and 5 consider the ADVANTAGES of the choice now written on their sheet and the secretary lists these.
- Groups 2, 4 and 6 consider the DISADVANTAGES of the choice now written on their sheet and the secretary lists these.
- When this has been done, groups 1 and 2, 3 and 4, and 5 and 6 amalgamate, examine the advantages and disadvantages that have been identified, and together decide on the likely outcomes.
- Give each group another sheet of paper to record these outcomes.
- Invite the groups to display their sheets and report to the class.
- These sheets can be left on display for reference purposes for the next phase.

Group Size: 5 - 6, 2 - 6
Time: 40 - 50 minutes
Materials: Each group requires:
- **FACTS ABOUT SMOKING**
- several large sheets of paper and a marker

Each student requires:
- **DECIDE ABOUT SMOKING**

• Phase III
- Give each student a copy of **DECIDE ABOUT SMOKING** and comment on how it is to be completed.
  - Identify your values regarding smoking, i.e. be clear about what is important to you and what you want. The results of Phase I will be useful here.
  - List the choices and consider the advantages/disadvantages and outcomes of each. Again, the results of Phase II will help.
  - If you feel ready to, make a decision which reflects your values and will help you achieve what you want.
  - Draw up a simple action plan to achieve this, i.e. what you can do now to ensure you get what you want.
- Allow time for students to complete this sheet.
- Students may work individually or in small self-selecting groups.
- Convene the class and discuss:
  - How did people feel about this session?
  - Did people find it difficult to complete the worksheet **DECIDE ABOUT SMOKING**? Why?
  - Is this a useful step-by-step procedure to follow?
  - How was it helpful?
  - Was everyone able to make a decision or did some feel they needed more information or to be clearer about their values?
  - Should this decision be expected to stand forever or might it change?
  - Why might this happen?
  - Some people smoke even though it is contrary to what they know is important to them. Why do you think this is?

- Why is it difficult to resist the influence of 'friends'?
- Is the person who puts pressure on you to do something you don't really want to do, a friend? Why?
- Do you have any tips for resisting influence but remaining accepted (i.e. not going along with the crowd)?

Extensions:

1. Explore the role of advertising and smoking. Is the glamour that surrounds smoking misleading? Are some of the facts missing? Make up adverts which show the harmful and dangerous side of smoking.
2. Students carry out a survey among relatives and friends collating evidence about smoking and people's habits. What decision did these people make? When was it made? Why? What do they consider the advantages and disadvantages of their decision, and the effect this decision has had on their lives? How do they feel now about this decision?
3. Invite students to debate the motion: SMOKING SHOULD BE BANNED IN OUR SOCIETY. Select two teams and give them time to prepare their arguments.
4. Students role-play a discussion taking place between a non-smoker, someone who smokes in moderation and a heavy smoker.
5. Show a video on the use of tobacco. The Health Education Service provides a range of good quality videos on smoking.
6. Explore ways to be assertive, i.e. to have the confidence to say what you believe, what you want and maintain the respect of others. Students could make a poster outlining suggestions for someone who has decided to be a non-smoker but wants to be accepted by his friends who are smokers.
7. In small groups, students take an aspect of smoking to research, e.g.
   The Law and Smoking
   Passive Smoking
   The Effect of Smoking on Your Heart
   Pregnancy and Smoking
   The History of Smoking

   These notes are put together in booklet form to make a class reference book.

Notes:

In the coming sessions, student will have the opportunity to apply the skills of decision making to situations in their own lives. The person who has thought about the issues and followed a decision-making strategy is more likely to make free and honest decisions and less likely to be influenced by peers or social pressures.

In this exercise, students are asked to make a decision on where they stand on the issue of smoking. The intention is not to influence *what* they decide but *how* they decide, i.e. the emphasis is on making a mature and conscious decision by following the decision-making process outlined earlier in this course.

Students may not feel 'ready' to make a decision (confused about their values - more time required - more information needed and so on) and this should be respected by the teacher.

Phase I helps the student to be clear about his values relating to smoking and is a crucial step in making an effective decision about smoking - a good decision will reflect the individual's values.

In Phase II, students inform themselves of the advantages/disadvantages and the consequences of these. The student will be helped in this by the worksheet **FACTS ABOUT SMOKING**. The teacher may wish to extend this phase by inviting students to research a particular aspect of the subject and make presentations to the class. The teacher may wish to make a formal presentation on smoking. Resources available from the local Health Education Service will be helpful in providing relevant information.

During Phase III, make obvious to the students how the design of the worksheet **DECIDE ABOUT SMOKING** reflects the elements of 'good' decision making that have been identified earlier in the course. The PLAN OF ACTION is intended to help the student consider practical ways of effecting this decision. For example, a person who has decided not to smoke might have as his plan:
1. To avoid people who might pressurise me to smoke.
2. Be prepared to say 'no'.

FACTS ABOUT SMOKING

When you smoke, your pulse increases by 10 - 20 strokes a minute.

Filters don't eliminate all the harmful substances that are in cigarettes.

Smokers are more likely to die of a heart attack than non-smokers.

Tobacco was introduced into England in the sixteenth century.

A smoker's risk of dying from lung cancer is 25 times greater than a non-smoker's.

Recent surveys show that the majority of smokers say they would like to give up.

It is illegal to sell tobacco to anyone below the age of 19.

Cigarette smoke is a mixture of over 2000 chemicals, many of which are harmful to health.

Tobacco smoke contains:
1 **NICOTINE**, which is addictive, makes the heart beat faster and raises blood pressure.
2 **CARBON MONOXIDE**, a poisonous gas which cuts down the amount of oxygen the blood can carry.
3 **TAR**, which collects in the lungs and contains substances which cause cancer.

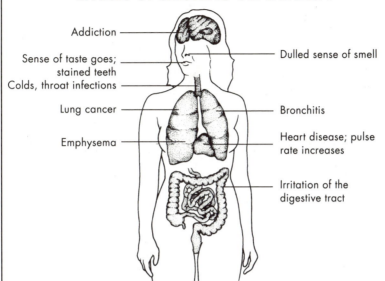

EFFECTS OF SMOKING ON THE BODY
- Addiction
- Sense of taste goes; stained teeth
- Colds, throat infections
- Lung cancer
- Emphysema
- Dulled sense of smell
- Bronchitis
- Heart disease; pulse rate increases
- Irritation of the digestive tract

Speech bubble (left): SMOKING MAKES ME FEEL SO GROWN UP. GIRLS LIKE SOMEONE WHO IS COOL.

Speech bubble (right): HIS BREATH SMELLS, THE SMOKE MAKES ME FEEL SICK, AND AFTER I'VE BEEN WITH HIM MY CLOTHES AND HAIR SMELL AWFUL.

'I'm in a wheelchair thanks to heavy cigarette smoking. They had to cut off my right leg because of bad circulation. The poor flow of blood caused gangrene to form in my foot.'

WARNING:

Passive smoking damages your health!

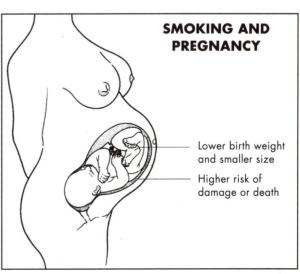

SMOKING AND PREGNANCY
- Lower birth weight and smaller size
- Higher risk of damage or death

A third of all smokers die between 10 - 15 years younger than non-smokers.

Smoking kills 274 people every day.

Every cigarette you smoke shortens your life by about 6 minutes.

Smokers have a low resistance to infection.

The risks of smoking decrease dramatically on giving up.

Out of 1000 smokers, about 6 will be killed in road accidents, but 250 will be killed by tobacco.

There are over 11 million ex-smokers in the UK.

A person who smokes 30 cigarettes a day inhales about 2 pints of tobacco tar in a year.

© Shay McConnon 1992

DECIDE ABOUT SMOKING

Name _____ Date _____

1 I want _____
(What is important to me in deciding whether to smoke?)

– to show off
– to be fit
– to feel relaxed
– to do what others do
– to save money
– to be seen as 'grown up'
– to be sociable
– the pleasure of smoking
– a long life
– a healthy life

2 Choices open to me

	ADVANTAGES	DISADVANTAGES	LIKELY OUTCOMES
To be a non-smoker			
To be a light smoker			
To be a heavy smoker			

3 What appears to be the best choice for getting what I want?
_____

4 My decision is _____

5 My plan of action is
(How can I achieve what I want?)

1 _____
2 _____
3 _____

Ⓟ © Shay McConnon 1992

8 DECIDE ABOUT ALCOHOL

Aim: To help students make an informed and considered decision about alcohol, using the decision-making strategy from this course.

Procedure:

• Phase I
- Form groups of 5 - 6 and decide on a spokesperson and secretary.
- Give each group a large sheet of paper and a marker.
- Students are to brainstorm the reasons why people choose to drink, i.e. what is important to them in deciding to drink.
- When this has been done, invite each group to report back and make a list of these responses on the blackboard or flipchart.
- Repeat this procedure, brainstorming the reasons why people choose not to drink, i.e. what is important to them in deciding not to drink.

• Phase II
- Form six groups (each group to consist of 2 - 6 students).
- Each group decides on a spokesperson and a secretary.
- Give each group the worksheet **FACTS ABOUT ALCOHOL** and explain that they may use this to complete the next task.
- Give each group a large sheet of paper and a marker.
- Groups 1 and 2 will consider the choice NOT TO DRINK (abstinence) and the secretary writes this at the top of the sheet.
- Groups 3 and 4 will consider TO DRINK A LITTLE (moderation) and write this at the top of the sheet.
- Groups 5 and 6 will consider TO DRINK A LOT (no limits) and write this at the top of the sheet.
- Groups 1, 3 and 5 consider the ADVANTAGES of the choice now written on their sheet and the secretary lists these.
- Groups 2, 4 and 6 consider the DISADVANTAGES of the choice now written on their sheet and the secretary lists these.
- When this has been done, groups 1 and 2, 3 and 4, and 5 and 6 amalgamate, examine the advantages and disadvantages that have been identified, and together decide on the likely outcomes.
- Give each group another large sheet of paper to record these outcomes.
- The other groups amalgamate and follow the same procedure.
- Invite the groups to display their sheets and report to the class.

Group Size: 5 - 6, 2 - 6

Time: 40 - 50 minutes

Materials: Each group requires:
- **FACTS ABOUT ALCOHOL**
- several large sheets of paper and a marker

Each student requires:
- **DECIDE ABOUT ALCOHOL**

- These sheets can be left on display for reference purposes for the next phase.

• Phase III
- Give each student a copy of **DECIDE ABOUT ALCOHOL** and comment on how it is to be completed.
  - Identify your values regarding alcohol, i.e. be clear about what is important to you and what you want. The results of Phase I will be useful here.
  - List the choices and consider the advantages/disadvantages and outcomes of each. Again, the results of Phase II will help.
  - If you feel able to, make a decision which reflects your values and will help you achieve what you want.
  - Draw up a simple action plan to achieve this, i.e. what you can do now to ensure you get what you want.
- Allow time for students to complete this sheet.
- Students may work individually or with people of their choosing.
- Convene the class and discuss:
  - How did people feel about this session?
  - Did people find it difficult to complete the worksheet **DECIDE ABOUT ALCOHOL**? Why?
  - Is this a useful step-by-step procedure to follow?
  - How did it help?
  - Was everyone able to make a decision or did some feel they needed more information or to be clearer about their values?
  - Should this decision be expected to stand forever or might it change?
  - Why might this happen?

Extensions:

1. Explore the role of advertising and alcohol. Is the glamour that surrounds the image of drinking misleading? Are some of the facts missing? Do the advertisements show people drunk, broken relationships, battered children, road accidents? Make up adverts which show the harmful and dangerous side of alcohol.
2. Students carry out a survey among relatives and friends collecting evidence about alcohol and people's habits. What decision did these people make? When was it made? Why? What do they consider the advantages and disadvantages of their decision, the effect this decision has had on their lives? How do they feel now about this decision and so on.
3. Invite students to debate the motion: ALCOHOL SHOULD BE BANNED IN OUR SOCIETY. Select two teams and give them time to prepare their arguments.
4. Students role-play a discussion taking place between a teetotaller, a moderate drinker and a heavy drinker.
5. Show a video on the use of alcohol. The Health Education Service provides a range of good quality videos on alcohol.
6. In small groups, students take an aspect of alcohol to research, e.g.
   Drinking and Driving
   The Alcoholic
   The Social Drinker
   Alcohol and The Law

   These notes are put together in booklet form to make a class reference book.

Notes:

The course continues to help students apply the skills of decision making to issues of concern in their lives.

Alcohol may or may not be an immediate issue with the young people in your class, but sooner or later they will have to make a decision: to drink or not, how much, where, when, and so on. Students are less likely to make a decision they will regret in the context of a party or with peer pressure if they have already considered the issues related to drinking alcohol.

The intention is not to influence what they decide but how they decide. Some students may not feel 'ready' to make a decision (confused about their values - more time needed - more information needed and so on) and this should be respected by the teacher.

Phase I helps the student to be clear about his values relating to alcohol and is a crucial step in making an effective decision about alcohol - a good decision will reflect the individual's values.

In Phase II, students inform themselves of the advantages/disadvantages and the consequences of these. The student will be helped in this by the worksheet **FACTS ABOUT ALCOHOL**. The teacher may wish to extend this phase by inviting students to research a particular aspect of the subject and make presentations to the class. The teacher may wish to make a formal presentation on alcohol. Resources available from the local Health Education Service will be helpful in providing relevant information.

During Phase III, make obvious to the students how the design of the worksheet **DECIDE ABOUT ALCOHOL** reflects the elements of 'good' decision making that have been identified earlier in the course. The PLAN OF ACTION is intended to help the student consider practical ways of effecting this decision. For example, a person who has decided to drink in moderation might have as his plan:
1. To set myself specific limits.
2. Not to go out with friends who drink heavily.
3. To make use of low-alcohol drinks.

DECIDE ABOUT ALCOHOL

FACTS ABOUT ALCOHOL

Hangovers are caused by drinking too much alcohol.

Alcohol is a chemical obtained by the fermentation of cereals, milk or fruit, or by distillation.

Peter died from asphyxiation due to vomit and acute alcoholic intoxication.

There is evidence that sensible drinking benefits your health.

33% of all offenders on probation were found to be problem drinkers.

The major cause of death for young males aged 17 to 24 is a road accident in which the victim has been drinking beforehand.

Alcohol is a drug - it alters the way the mind and body work.

Alcohol is a contributory factor in 33% of all child abuse cases.

The liver can only burn up one standard drink in an hour.

HEAVY DRINKING OVER MANY YEARS LEADS TO...

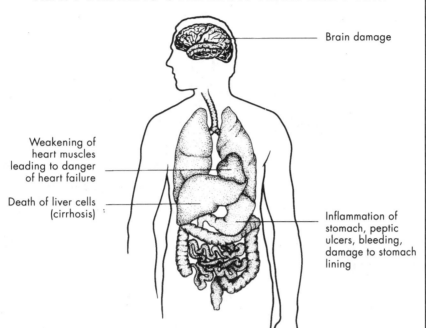

- Brain damage
- Weakening of heart muscles leading to danger of heart failure
- Death of liver cells (cirrhosis)
- Inflammation of stomach, peptic ulcers, bleeding, damage to stomach lining

1 or 2 DRINKS
Skin flushes
Inhibitions disappear
Heart speeds up

3 DRINKS
Judgement slows down
Giddiness
Lack of co-ordination

5 DRINKS
Vision blurs
Speech slurs
Reactions slow

8 DRINKS
Staggering
Loss of balance
Double vision

20 DRINKS
Unconsciousness

26 DRINKS
DEATH DUE TO ALCOHOLIC POISONING

The suicide rate among alcoholics is 80 times greater than among the rest of the population.

1 UNIT =

half pint of beer = 1 single whisky = 1 glass of wine = 1 glass sherry

Sensible drinking limits

 WOMEN - up to 14 units in a week.

 MEN - up to 21 units in a week.

Alcohol costs industry £1600 million a year.

About one third of all accidents in the home are related to drinking.

It is illegal to sell alcohol to people under the age of 18.

The effects of alcohol depend on how much you drink, your height, age, weight and sex and whether you have eaten recently.

Small amounts of alcohol can help digestion.

An alcoholic is someone who is physically or psychologically dependent on alcohol.

Heavy drinkers can suffer DTs - they think they are being watched by imaginary creatures.

Alcohol is absorbed directly into the bloodstream.

Look at it this way - you're actually giving your baby an alcoholic drink if you are pregnant and drink alcohol.

Alcohol is a major cause of road traffic accidents.

© Shay McConnon 1992

DECIDE ABOUT ALCOHOL

Name _____ Date _____

– to show off
– to be fit and healthy
– to feel relaxed

1 I want _____
(What is important to me in deciding whether to drink?)

– to do what others do
– to save money
– to be seen as 'grown up'
– to be sociable
– to enjoy the pleasure of alcohol
– to forget my problems

2 Choices open to me

	ADVANTAGES	DISADVANTAGES	LIKELY OUTCOMES
To be teetotal			
To be a moderate drinker			
To be a heavy drinker			

3 What appears to be the best choice for getting what I want?
_____

4 My decision is _____

5 My plan of action is
(How can I achieve what I want?)

1 _____
2 _____
3 _____

Ⓟ © Shay McConnon 1992

DECIDE ABOUT DRUGS

Aim: To help students make an informed and considered decision about illicit drugs, using the decision-making strategy from this course.

Procedure:

• Phase I
- Form groups of 5 - 6 and decide on a spokesperson and secretary.
- Give each group a large sheet of paper and a marker.
- Students are to brainstorm the reasons why people choose to take illegal drugs, i.e. what is important to them in deciding to take drugs.
- When this has been done, invite each group to report back and make a list of these responses on the blackboard or flipchart.
- Repeat this procedure, brainstorming the reasons why people choose not to take drugs, i.e. what is important to them in deciding not to take drugs.

• Phase II
- Form six groups (each group to consist of 2 - 6 students).
- Each group decides on a spokesperson and a secretary.
- Give each group the worksheet **FACTS ABOUT DRUGS** and explain that they may use this to complete the next task.
- Give each group a large sheet of paper and a marker.
- Groups 1 and 2 will consider the choice 'NO' TO ILLEGAL DRUGS and the secretary writes this at the top of the sheet.
- Groups 3 and 4 will consider 'YES' TO SOME DRUGS and write this at the top of the sheet.
- Groups 5 and 6 will consider 'YES' TO ALL DRUGS and write this at the top of the sheet.
- Groups 1, 3 and 5 consider the ADVANTAGES of the choice now written on their sheet and the secretary lists these.
- Groups 2, 4 and 6 consider the DISADVANTAGES of the choice now written on their sheet and the secretary lists these.
- When this has been done, groups 1 and 2, 3 and 4, and 5 and 6 amalgamate, examine the advantages and disadvantages that have been identified, and together decide on the likely outcomes.
- The other groups amalgamate and follow the same procedure.
- Give each group another large sheet of paper to write these outcomes on.
- Invite each group to display their sheets and report to the class.
- These sheets can be left on display for reference purposes for the next phase.

Group Size: 5 - 6, 2 - 6
Time: 40 - 50 minutes
Materials: Each group requires:
- **FACTS ABOUT DRUGS**
- several large sheets of paper and a marker

Each student requires:
- **DECIDE ABOUT DRUGS**

• Phase III
- Give each student a copy of **DECIDE ABOUT DRUGS** and comment on how it is to be completed.
  - Identify your values regarding illegal drugs, i.e. be clear about what is important to you and what you want. The results of Phase I will be useful here.
  - List the choices and consider the advantages/disadvantages and outcomes of each. Again, the results of Phase II will help.
  - If you feel ready to, make a decision which reflects your values and will help you achieve what you want.
  - Draw up a simple action plan to achieve this, i.e. what you can do now to ensure you get what you want.
- Allow time for students to complete this sheet.
- Students may work individually or with people of their choosing.
- Convene the class and discuss:
  - How did people feel about this session?
  - Was everyone able to make a decision or did some feel they needed more information or to be clearer about their values?
  - Should this decision be expected to stand forever or might it change?
  - Why might this happen?

Extensions:

1 Give each student 2 - 3 slips of paper and invite them to write questions they would like to ask on illicit drugs. These are collected and used by the teacher as the basis for a presentation on drugs.

2. Show a video on illicit drugs. The Health Education Service provides a range of good quality videos.
3. Students role-play a situation between two friends: A has been offered drugs and is thinking seriously of saying 'yes'. B is A's best friend and tries to dissuade A from starting.
4. Solvent abuse is a form of drug taking and the teacher may wish to complete a parallel exercise with the students on solvent abuse.
5. In small groups students take an aspect of drug abuse to research, e.g.
   Drug Dependency
   Drugs and The Law
   The Drug Pusher
   Drug Rehabilitation

   These notes are put together in booklet form to make a class reference book.

Notes:

This session is concerned with illicit drugs and not with prescribed or socially accepted drugs.

The intention is to help students become aware of the issues involved in drug taking along with their personal values in so far as they relate to this issue and then attempt a conscious and informed decision about illicit drugs using the decision-making strategy identified earlier in the course.

Some of the information about illicit drugs is technical and the teacher may need time to find the answers to students' questions. Encourage the students to become involved in finding the answers themselves and make available a variety of leaflets, posters and information sheets from the Health Education Service.

Because of the complex nature of this subject, students may require extra time to get relevant information, to consider the alternatives and look at the consequences of drug issues. The teacher may wish to spread this strategy over several sessions.

Some students may not feel 'ready' to make a decision (confused about their values - more time needed - more information needed and so on) and this should be respected by the teacher.

This exercise is parallel to the preceding ones. Students identify their values (what is important to them in deciding whether to use drugs), inform themselves and weigh up the pros and cons of the choices open to them.

DECIDE ABOUT DRUGS

FACTS ABOUT DRUGS

For the purposes of this lesson, we are talking about drugs used illegally, such as heroin, cannabis, magic mushrooms, amphetamines, LSD, crack, and cocaine.

'Drugs are about as glamorous as cancer'

The drug taker often starts to take greater doses to get bigger kicks.

Most drugs are poisons.

One LSD tripper jumped out of a ten-storey window and fell to his death on the street below. He thought he could fly.

A single dose of just one pure gram of cocaine can kill.

Under pressure, ex-addicts often return to drug-taking.

A drug is any substance that acts upon the central nervous system.

The combination of drugs with alcohol can result in death.

"I got AIDS from sharing a needle with someone who was infected."

"Look at me. My life is over at 20: no money, no job, no friends, no future." A heroin addict.

HOW DRUGS CAN AFFECT A PERSON'S LIFE

Health
Drugs can damage the body in many ways:
– heart failure
– infection
– hepatitis
– weight loss
– sores
some users risk AIDS, mental illness or even death.

Work
Drugs affect a person's ability to work and concentrate. Classroom performance suffers and workers risk being sacked.

Life
Drug users can be lethargic, with little interest in life, in being successful or in looking to the future.

Relationships
Drugs can make a person moody and depressed. This can cause a great strain on relationships and family break-ups.

Crime
It usually takes larger and larger doses to get the same 'kick' from drugs. Addicts often turn to crime to get the money for these... mugging, drug dealing, shoplifting, and prostitution.

"Until he started taking drugs, he was a boy with a promising future," said the judge who sentenced him yesterday at Manchester Crown Court.

When Julia's baby was born he was already a heroin addict - just like his mum.

Peter was found dead in his bed this morning from an overdose of heroin.

Even if you do not take any more LSD, hallucinations can return days, weeks or months later.

First time heroin users can be violently sick.

To make greater profits, dealers often add substances like talcum powder, chalk, brick and glass dust to the drugs to make them go further.

DRUG	WHAT THEY DO	EFFECTS	DEPENDENCE
Barbiturates	depress the functioning of the brain	drowsiness, sleep, depression - user sometimes lapses into coma and dies	physical & psychological dependence is strong
Amphetamines	stimulate the nervous system	depression, exhaustion - sometimes visual distortion/ feeling of persecution	psychological dependence sometimes quick & strong
L.S.D.	changes sensory perception e.g. taker thinks s/he can fly off a high building	bad 'trips' can cause depression and dizziness - hallucinating people are accident prone, resulting in serious injury or even death	psychological dependence develops if drug used a lot
Cannabis	affects the user's ability to judge space, distance and time	risk of accidents increases - can lead to anxiety, elation, confusion and paranoid ideas	some people develop psychological dependence
Heroin	depresses the activity of the nervous system and dilutes blood vessels	extreme physical and mental deterioration	physical & psychological dependence develops early and is strong
Cocaine	heart rate and blood pressure increase - visual distortions - hallucinations	loss of appetite, behaviour changes - physical deterioration	psychological dependence is very strong

DRUGS HELPLINES — If you want confidential advice, dial 100 and ask for "Freefone Drug Problems" for information about local drug advice centres.

© Shay McConnon 1992

DECIDE ABOUT DRUGS

Name _____ Date _____

1 I want _____
(What is important to me in deciding whether to take drugs?)

– to be law abiding
– to show off
– to be fit and healthy
– to escape from problems
– to feel relaxed
– to rebel
– to get attention
– to save money
– to be accepted by others
– to be seen as 'hard'
– to satisfy curiosity
– to take risks

2 Choices open to me

	ADVANTAGES	DISADVANTAGES	LIKELY OUTCOMES
To say 'no' to all illegal drugs			
To say 'yes' to some illegal drugs			
To say 'yes' to all illegal drugs			

3 What appears to be the best choice for getting what I want?
_____
_____

4 My decision is _____

5 My plan of action is
(How can I achieve what I want?)

1 _____

2 _____

3 _____

Ⓟ © Shay McConnon 1992

10 DECIDE YOUR CAREER

Aim: To help students along the path to an informed and conscious decision about their future careers.

Procedure:

● Phase I
- Form groups of 5 - 6 and decide on a spokesperson and a secretary.
- Give each group a large sheet of paper and a marker.
- Students are to brainstorm the sort of things which are important to people in choosing a job or career.
- When this has been done, invite each group to report back and list their findings on the blackboard or flipchart.

● Phase II
- Give each student a copy of **DECIDE YOUR CAREER**.
- From the list on the blackboard and the clues on the worksheet, students write what is important to them personally in choosing a job or career and list three choices which might satisfy these.
- Form groups of 3 - 4.
- Students take it in turns to be the focal person.
- The focal person, in consultation with the other members of the group, lists the advantages/disadvantages and likely outcomes of each career decision and writes these on the worksheet.
- Students then complete the remainder of the worksheet.
- Convene the class and discuss:
  – How easy/difficult is it to make a decision about your future career?
  – Why is this?
  – How important a decision is this? Why?
  – Is it realistic to be thinking about a career decision?
  – How can an 'informed' decision be made, i.e. how can people get the information to help them make a mature decision?
  – Are you likely to change your mind?
  – Is it important to keep your career options open?
  – What sort of information is required?
  – Who in the school can help you make a good career choice?

Extensions:
1. Explore opportunities for boys, and girls in terms of careers. Are there still 'mens jobs' and 'womens jobs'? Should there be?
2. In small self-selecting groups, students list their strengths, abilities, skills and preferences. This is then used as an aid in helping the student make a career decision.
3. Students list the advantages/disadvantages/ outcomes of 'A' levels, YTS, vocational courses, a casual job, unemployment, and so on.

Group Size: 5 - 6, 3 - 4
Time: 30 - 40 minutes
Materials: Each group requires:
- a large sheet of paper and a marker

Each student requires:
- the worksheet **DECIDE YOUR CAREER**

Notes:

Students are often worried and confused about a career choice, especially as the range of careers can be daunting, the decision may not be immediate and students may be unsure of a strategy for decision making. This exercise allows students to practise applying the skills of decision making to a 'good' choice of career. A single session of 30 - 40 minutes is limited and the teacher may wish to spend additional time on this subject.

Although some students will have a clear idea about the career they would like to follow, many are likely to change their minds. This makes it important for them to keep their options open to take advantage of different career opportunities.

This exercise is parallel to the preceding ones. Students identify their values (what is important to them in choosing a career), inform themselves and weigh up the advantages and disadvantages of several choices of career.

DECIDE YOUR CAREER

Name _____ Date _____

1 What I want in a job/career is:

_____
_____
_____
_____
_____
_____

RESPONSIBILITY
PROMOTION
OVERTIME
FRIENDLY WORKMATES
SECURITY
JOB SATISFACTION
A GOOD BOSS
TRAINING
ACCOMMODATION
A CHALLENGE
A GOOD SALARY

2 Career choices

	ADVANTAGES	DISADVANTAGES	LIKELY OUTCOMES

3 What appears to be the best choice for getting what I want?
_____

4 How can I get more information about this career?
_____
_____

5 What further training/qualifications will I need?
_____
_____

6 Here is my plan for achieving this:

a _____
b _____
c _____

© Shay McConnon 1992

11 DECIDE YOUR SUBJECTS

Aim: To help students make a decision about subject options.

Procedure:

● **Phase I**
○ Form groups of 5 - 6 and decide on a spokesperson and a secretary.
○ Give each group a large sheet of paper and a marker.
○ Groups are to list what is important in making a successful decision about subject options.
○ After 5 - 6 minutes, convene the class and invite each group to report back.
○ Discuss:
  – What subjects are compulsory?
  – Can you make a good decision if you are not clear about your career?
  – Students' ideas about careers change. How can you cater for this in your choice of subjects?
  – How important is it to choose subjects you enjoy?
  – What about those subjects which develop your talents and skills?

● **Phase II**
○ Give each student the worksheet **GET IT RIGHT!**
○ Comment on this sheet and how it is to be completed.
○ Students may work on their own or in self-selecting groups.
○ When this has been done, form groups of 3 - 4.
○ Students take it in turns to be the focal person. The focal person checks out with the other members, their answers to the questions listed in Section B of the worksheet.
○ If the answer is YES, the focal person writes Y in the box. If the answer is NO, N is written and P for PERHAPS.
○ Students now complete the remaining sections of the worksheet.

● **Phase III**
○ Convene the class and discuss:
  – How helpful has this session been?
  – Should your choice depend on whether you like or dislike the teacher? Why?
  – Should your decision be influenced by your friend's choice of subjects? Why?
  – Are there such things as girls' or boys' subjects?
  – Should you choose only those subjects you find easy?
  – Should you choose only those subjects you enjoy?
  – What would you say to someone who says, 'I don't need to keep my options open: I know what job I want'?
  – Where can you get help in deciding on your subject options?

Extension:

Students make a list of subjects and grade them according to various criteria, e.g. 'subjects I like', 'subjects I find interesting', 'my favourite subjects', 'subjects I am good at', and so on. These can be given a score 0 -10.

Group Size: 5 - 6
Time: 30 - 40 minutes
Materials: Each student requires:
○ the worksheet **GET IT RIGHT!**
Each group requires:
○ a large sheet of paper and a marker

Notes:

Having identified a career choice, students now look at an intermediary step in achieving this: subject options. A single session of 30 - 40 minutes is limited and the teacher may wish to spend additional time on this subject.

Students are often confused and worried about their subject choices and how this may affect their future career. Students should be encouraged to get the balance right, rather than concentrate too much on one subject area. This has the advantage of leaving career and educational options open.

Warn against choosing a subject just because a friend has chosen it, or because you like or dislike the teacher or because you think certain subjects are only for boys or only for girls.

DECIDE YOUR SUBJECTS

GET IT RIGHT

Name _____ Date _____

SECTION A

List of subjects	Compulsory subjects	Subjects which are important to my choice of career	Subjects I enjoy	Subjects which develop my talents and interests (usually the subjects I am best at)	My choices

SECTION B

Check out your choice of subjects with the other people in your group. If they feel the answer to a question is YES write Y in the box; if they feel NO write N, and P for PARTLY/PERHAPS.

a Does it fit in with your career aspirations?

b Does it develop your skills and interests?

c Does it allow you to change your ideas about a career?

d Are there subjects from a variety of areas (e.g. science, language, humanities)?

e Are they subjects you enjoy?

WHAT THE GROUP THINKS	WHAT I THINK

I am happy about my choice of subjects.   I am not happy about my choice of subjects.

℗ © Shay McConnon 1992

12 DECIDE ABOUT...

Aim: To give students the opportunity to use a decision-making strategy to help them achieve greater personal effectiveness.

Procedure:

● Phase I
- Give each student a copy of **ME!**
- Comment on this sheet and how it is to be completed.
- Explain that it is important for students to be honest in completing this sheet - it is a personal exercise to help them identify areas in their lives where they would like to be more successful.
- Allow time for students to complete this sheet and identify two areas where they would like to be more successful.

● Phase II
- Students with the same or similar 'goals' now form groups of 3 - 4.
- Give each student a copy of **DECIDE ABOUT...**
- Explain that this follows the decision-making structure used in earlier strategies.
- In their groups, students take it in turns to say what is important to them about this issue. For example, the values surrounding a decision about 'Completing my homework' might be success in examinations, getting a good job/decent wage, and so on.
- Students complete part 1 of the worksheet.
- In their groups, students now brainstorm different ways to achieve what they want.
- Groups could appoint a secretary who lists these alternatives on the back of the worksheet **ME!**
- From this list, each student chooses the three alternatives which he feels are most advantageous to achieving his goal. (This is to be an individual, not a group, decision.)
- These alternatives are noted in part 2 of the worksheet and students then write the advantages/disadvantages/likely outcomes of each. (Students may work together on this.)
- Reflecting on these alternatives, students complete part 3 of the worksheet.
- In their groups, students take it in turns to read aloud their decisions and ask other group members for suggestions on realising them.
- These are noted on part 4.

Group Size: 3 - 4
Time: 30 - 40 minutes
Materials: Each student requires:
- the worksheets **ME!** and **DECIDE ABOUT...**

Notes:
This exercise allows students to identify areas in their lives where they would like to be more successful and then decide on ways to achieve these goals.

The worksheet **ME!** allows students to appraise themselves in the listed areas. These headings are a selection of social and life skills which can be varied to suit the needs of specific individuals or groups.

Phase II shows how the decision-making strategy used in earlier exercises can be applied by students to achieve their goals. It is a tool they can use to achieve success. The teacher may wish to make available to students copies of **DECIDE ABOUT...** to use in other areas of their lives. Encourage students to work together, support each other, review progress and, if necessary, decide on different alternatives to help them achieve what they want.

● Phase III
- Convene the class and discuss:
  - How helpful has this session been?
  - Are people optimistic that they can achieve what they want?
  - What can you do if you are not successful?
  - How can students help each other to be successful?
  - Can this decision-making technique be used in other ways? Examples?

Extension:
Make available **SELF-CONTRACT** and **SUCCESS** worksheets contained in other books in the series to interested students.

DECIDE ABOUT...

ME!

Name _____   Date _____

	Success rating out of ten	Continue as I am	Like to change
Making friends			
Talking to the opposite sex			
Keeping a conversation going			
Expressing my opinion			
Keeping my temper			
Making complaints			
Working in a group or team			
Managing my time			
Being liked by others			
Completing my homework			
Getting on with teachers			
Keeping out of trouble			
Handling boredom			
Feeling stressed			
Getting on with Mum and/or Dad			
Being organised			

KEEPING MY TEMPER

MANAGING MY TIME

a Note your success rating in the first column, e.g. if you make friends easily give yourself a high score, (10 = high). If you have difficulty in making friends, give yourself a low score (1 = low).

b Tick in the second column those areas you do not wish to change.

c Tick in the third column those areas you wish to change and star the boxes.

3 stars to indicate what is extremely important to you
2 stars to indicate what is very important to you
1 star to indicate what is important to you.

I would like to be more successful in:

1 _____

2 _____

3 _____

KEEPING OUT OF TROUBLE

℗ © Shay McConnon 1992

DECIDE ABOUT...

Name _____ Date _____

1 I want _____
(What is important to me about this issue)

2 Choices open to me
(different ways of achieving what I want)

	ADVANTAGES	DISADVANTAGES	LIKELY OUTCOMES

3 What appears to be the best choice for getting what I want?
_____

4 My decision is _____

5 My plan of action is   1 _____
(How can I achieve what I want?)
                                          2 _____

                                          3 _____

© Shay McConnon 1992

13 HOW HAVE WE GOT ON?

Aim: To review the course on Making Decisions and to assess the student's response to it.

Procedure:

• Phase I
- Divide the class into two circles, an inner and an outer circle, with the students facing each other in pairs.
- Tell the students to discuss: 'What I liked about this course' with their partners.
- Allow 2 - 3 minutes for this.
- Inner circle moves to the left and students now discuss: 'What I disliked about this course'.
- Continue this procedure with the following discussion topics:
  - Why I enjoyed/didn't enjoy this course
  - Suggestions I have for improving the course
  - The most important thing I have learnt probably is...
  - The skills I consider important to making decisions are...
  - I am good at making decisions because...

• Phase II
- Give each student the worksheet **HOW HAVE I GOT ON?**
- Comment as necessary.
- Students are to complete these working individually.
- The completed sheets are collected and handed to the teacher.

Extensions:
1. Turn the phrases on the worksheet into questions, e.g. 'Did you enjoy the course - a lot? a bit? not at all?' etc. and write each question on a large sheet of paper. Display these around the room. Students are to wander around the room answering the questions by writing on the sheets of paper. Conclude by commenting on each sheet and inviting further comments.
2. Students complete and share a list of incomplete sentences which will help them review the course, e.g. 'I liked this course because...', 'I am please I did...', 'I would like to do more of...', 'I learned...'.

Group Size: Varies
Time: 30 - 40 minutes
Materials: Each student requires:
- worksheet **HOW HAVE I GOT ON?**

Notes:

Evaluation is an essential function in any education programme. It enables teachers to monitor progress and provides them with feedback on the effectiveness of the programme, course materials and strategies. Ideally, evaluation should be regarded as a continuous process and not an isolated procedure tackled at the end of the course.

Young people are inclined to find evaluation difficult and a written questionnaire often gets limited results. So Phase I begins with an activity intended to stimulate students' memories, feelings and judgement. This is then followed by the questionnaire.

HOW HAVE I GOT ON?

Name _____   Date _____

I have found this course useful:

very   not at all
└───┴───┴───┴───┴───┘

I have enjoyed this course:

a lot   not at all
└───┴───┴───┴───┴───┘

CIRCLE THE WORDS YOU FEEL APPLY TO THE COURSE

confusing   easy   helpful   stressful   stimulating

difficult   relaxing   fun   relevant

disappointing   depresssing   irrelevant   entertaining   interesting

Two things I disliked about the course:

1 _____

2 _____

Two things I liked about the course:

1 _____

2 _____

Rate the following: very useful   not at all

worksheets   └───┴───┴───┴───┴───┘
discussion   └───┴───┴───┴───┴───┘
teacher talking └───┴───┴───┴───┴───┘
video (if used) └───┴───┴───┴───┴───┘
role-play   └───┴───┴───┴───┴───┘

Probably the most important thing I have learnt is:

_____
_____

The goals I have set myself are:

_____
_____

My suggestions for improving the course are:

_____
_____

I am good at making decisions because:

_____
_____

The steps which are important to making a decision are:

_____
_____
_____
_____

© Shay McConnon 1992